MW01580922

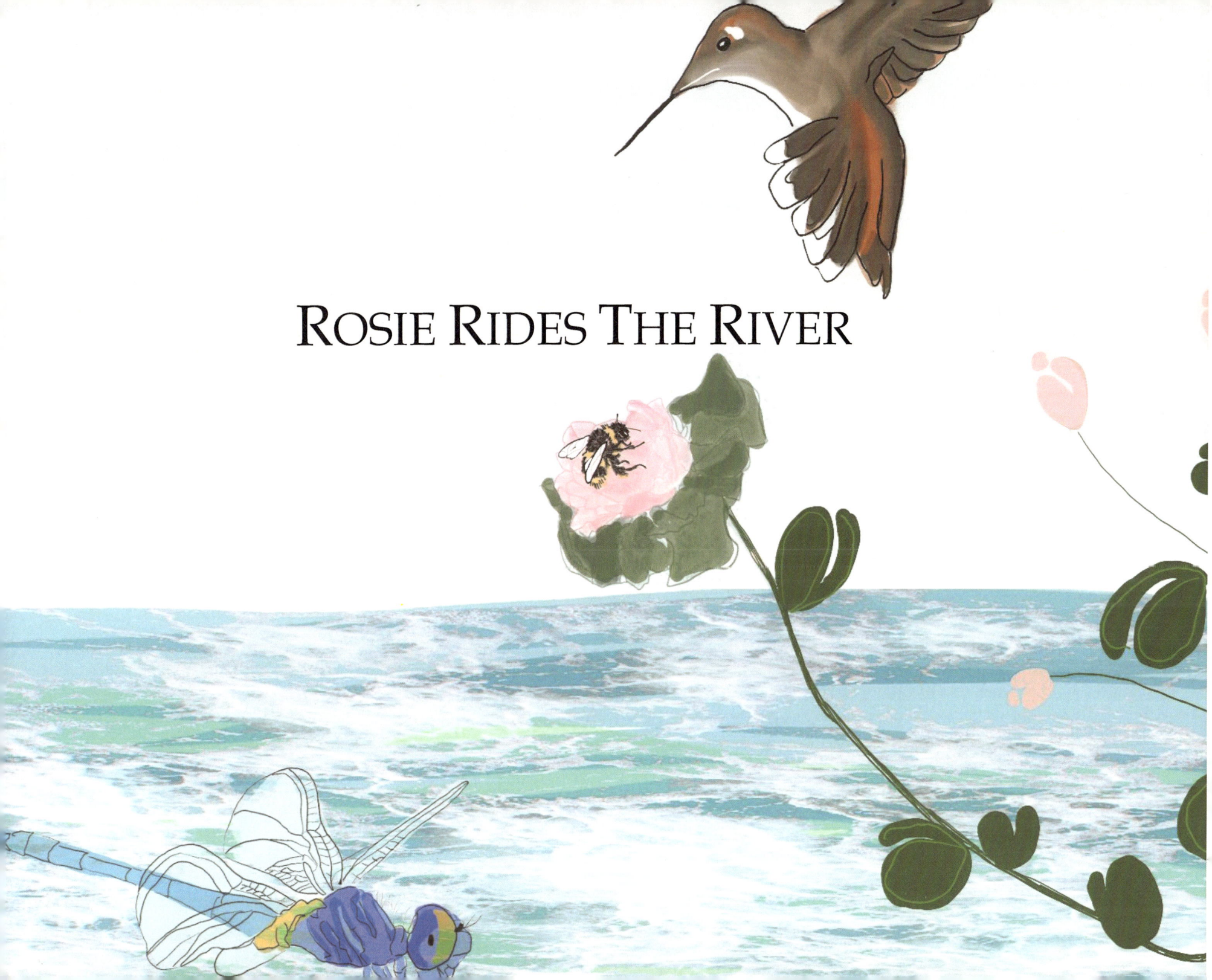

# ROSIE RIDES THE RIVER

©2021 Y. Niki Rainwater

"Rosie Rides The River" by Niki Rainwater. Published by H&H Publishing.

No part of this publication may be reproduced in whole or in part, or stored in a retrieval system, or transmitted in any

 form or by any means, electronic, mechanical, photocopying, recording,

or otherwise without written permission by the publisher/author. For information regarding permission, write to

 nikijrainwater@gmail.com

ISBN: 978-1-7367757-0-7

Text and illustration copyright © 2021 by Niki Rainwater. Cover by Taylor Blacklock.

*For Tenzing and Trinley*

*And all the Hummingbirds and Dragonflies*

*In loving memory of my mother, Gail*

-Niki Rainwater

*For my mom, who always encouraged me to be my most creative self.*

-Taylor Blacklock

*F*or as long as anyone could remember, Great Grandfather Granite had been the guardian of the wild river. He stood tall and mighty and held the river with strong arms as the water rushed through his rocky fingers, dancing, singing, crashing. He watched over the forest in silence, as he had done for hundreds of years, speaking but rarely. Great Grandfather Granite loved all the creatures of the forest: insects, reptiles, birds and beasts. Most of all, he loved the fragrance of the wild roses. This made him smile, shaking loose bits of rock which tumbled down his cheeks and fell into the river below.

Along the banks of the wild river, there lived the sweetest smelling roses in all the forest. The rose vines grew in a wild and tangly way. Tiny pink rosebuds peeped out from the tangle and sipped from the mist that swirled up from the rushing river. On the biggest vine, one very long stem pushed its way through the tangles, stretching out over the wild water. At its tip grew the tiniest wild rosebud, named Rosie.

On a late spring afternoon, a family hiking by the river stopped to smell the sweet wild roses that grew along the riverbank. The sound of the children's laughter tickled Rosie. Each following day became longer and warmer. More and more hikers stopped to smell the roses. Sometimes they would stay to picnic, or just watch the river for a little while before moving on. Each day Rosie looked forward to seeing the children who visited the rose vines. She never grew tired of their joyful squeals and belly laughs.

From her prickly perch above the river, Rosie grew and grew, until one day two of her petals opened and she could see all around. She watched as the river roared below her, spraying mist into the air. She reached out with her petals to catch a bit of the water, but it was beyond her reach.

Zwoosh! Suddenly, a little bird swooped into the mist fluttering so close that he splashed her. "Do you want to play with me?" asked the little bird.

"Yes!" answered Rosie as she shook the water from her petals.

The little bird twirled and zoomed in and out of the wild river mist, flying circles around the tiny pink rosebud.

The two new friends laughed and played all day long,. Rosie wished that she too could move through the air.

In the coming days, one by one, all of the tiny pink rosebud's petals opened and she was a rosebud no more. She was a rose!

How she longed to be able to fly high above the river like the little bird. She wanted to chase circles around him and dive into the mist just like he did.

*I wish I could fly so I could make others as happy as the little bird makes me,* thought Rosie.

"Will you teach me how to fly?" she asked her new friend.

The little bird cocked his head and thought for a minute before answering. "Rosie, I found you because of your beautiful smell. Because of you, the river and the forest smell like happiness! I wish I could smell as sweet as you!" said the little bird.

"But I want to fly through the air as you do! Think of the adventures we might have," cried Rosie.

She soon began to notice that other creatures of the

forest lifted their noses high as

they passed by her vine. Sometimes they even poked

their noses into her petals to be closer to her lovely

scent. The bees came to visit Rosie to share their

daily news. The hummingbirds and dragonflies would

zip in close to ask for a sip of the tiny rose's sweet

nectar and then flash away quickly.

Still, Rosie thought about flying over the river and seeing the world beyond the forest.

The other tiny pink wild roses were content with life on the tangled green vines. Try as they did, they could not understand why their sister would want to fly away.

Early one morning when the little bird and Rosie were playing, she felt something move inside her stem. As she bent down to take a look, her stem snapped and a gust of wind carried her straight up into the air. She was flying! The little bird dived and caught Rosie right as she was about to splash into the wild river.

Up, up, up they flew. It seemed the tiny pink rose could see everything! The rose vines below, the great river boulders, the treetops. The wind raced through her petals. The two friends soared over a waterfall, past Great-Grandfather Granite's rocky face. He smiled as the scent of the wild rose drifted up into his nose and made the ferns in his nostrils quiver.

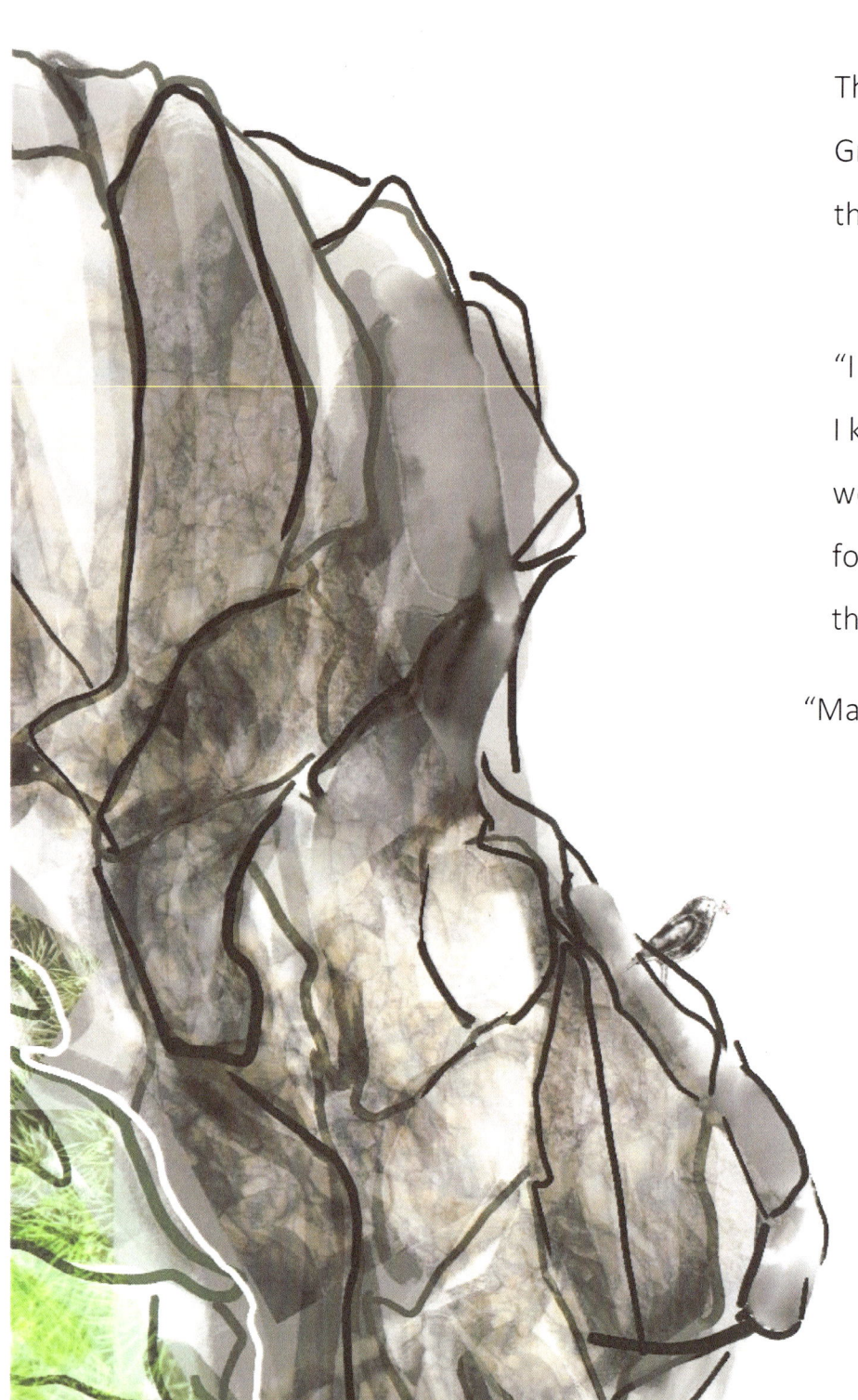

The little bird and Rosie soon found a spot upon Great Grandfather Granite's nose where they could rest. "What did you think of flying?" the little bird asked Rosie.

"I loved seeing so many beautiful things," she answered, "but now I know flying is for birds, not for roses." And in hearing her own words, Rosie became sad. She missed the children she had grown fond of on the riverbank. She still wanted to see the world beyond the forest more than ever, but how?

"Maybe you could try floating?" the little bird offered.

"I would like to try," said Rosie.

The last rays of sunlight fell across Great-Grandfather Granite's tall, chiseled face. His heart was warmed by the voices of the wild rose and bird resting on his nose.

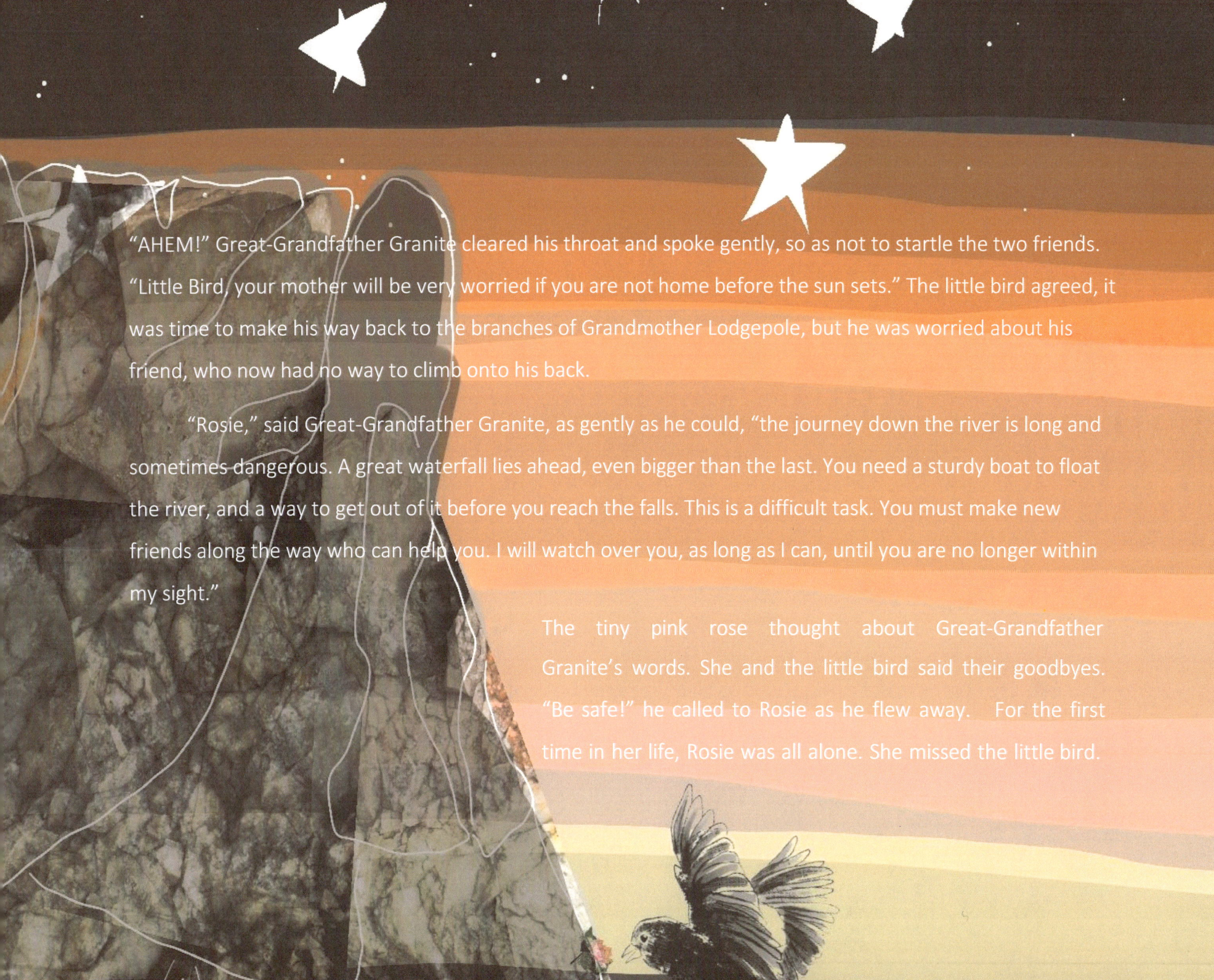

"AHEM!" Great-Grandfather Granite cleared his throat and spoke gently, so as not to startle the two friends. "Little Bird, your mother will be very worried if you are not home before the sun sets." The little bird agreed, it was time to make his way back to the branches of Grandmother Lodgepole, but he was worried about his friend, who now had no way to climb onto his back.

"Rosie," said Great-Grandfather Granite, as gently as he could, "the journey down the river is long and sometimes dangerous. A great waterfall lies ahead, even bigger than the last. You need a sturdy boat to float the river, and a way to get out of it before you reach the falls. This is a difficult task. You must make new friends along the way who can help you. I will watch over you, as long as I can, until you are no longer within my sight."

The tiny pink rose thought about Great-Grandfather Granite's words. She and the little bird said their goodbyes. "Be safe!" he called to Rosie as he flew away. For the first time in her life, Rosie was all alone. She missed the little bird.

Mother Moon made her silent journey in the sky above the aspens as Rosie fell asleep beneath Great-Grandfather Granite's watchful eye.

With the stars twinkling overhead, the tiny pink rose dreamed about a place where the river was wide and calm. In her dream, children played along the banks, their voices floating in the air, drifting out over the water. The sound was sweet music to the tiny pink rose.

There was a little island in the center of the river, covered in forget-me-nots and tiny yellow roses.

Rosie was still smiling in her sleep as Father Sun began to slowly awaken the forest:


"Tiny rose so pink and bright,

Your petals open to the light.

The river flows beneath your branch,

Running, leaping, in its dance!

You long to see what lies beyond,

Perhaps you'll find a quiet pond?

Brave as the river,

From here on after,

Listen for the children's laughter."

Rosie awoke and knew just what to do. She remembered the hikers who had visited her vine and the sound of the children's laughter. She had to find the place where children played. She wanted to hear their music again. The tiny rose shook the dew from her petals, which startled a mama lizard that had been resting beside her in the early morning sun.

"Good morning, Little One," the lizard said.

"Good morning, Mrs. Lizard," answered Rosie politely.

"Many creatures stop here for a sun bath, but never before have I seen a flower resting here," said Mrs. Lizard.

I wanted to learn to fly and go on an adventure with my friend, the little bird." Then Rosie asked Mrs. Lizard if she knew if there was such a place as Forget-Me-Not Island.

"Yes, there is," Mrs. Lizard answered, "I'm going there to lay my eggs. First, I must stop at the great falls to catch some bugs for my breakfast."

The tiny pink rose became very excited. "Can you please take me with you?" she asked. To this Mrs. Lizard agreed. She helped Rosie wiggle onto her back and the two made their way down the river path. Great Grandfather Granite smiled and said farewell to the two new friends.

Rosie marveled at the warmth of the sunlit path, and at the many different kinds of markings etched into the dust. Rosie saw that Mrs. Lizard's footprints left a pattern of tiny stars in the dirt as they walked along. She thought of the stars that glimmered in the night sky, high above the branch upon which she was born. When they reached the great falls, Mrs. Lizard wished the tiny rose a safe journey and began the task of catching bugs with her long, swift tongue. Rosie thanked Mrs. Lizard and said goodbye.

The great falls were even bigger and noisier than those Rosie had lived above on her vine, and far more dangerous, should she fall in. Before Rosie could think another thought, a huge tree trunk came charging downriver and spilled over the falls, taking her with it! Rosie hung on for dear life before jumping into a knot hole. She closed her eyes tight and burrowed deep inside.

"Wooo Hooo! Hello there, Tiny Rose!" The voice was one she had heard before.

"Ponderosa?! What are you doing here?" shouted Rosie, amid the roar of the falls. "A beaver family needs my help

d
o
w
n
s
t r

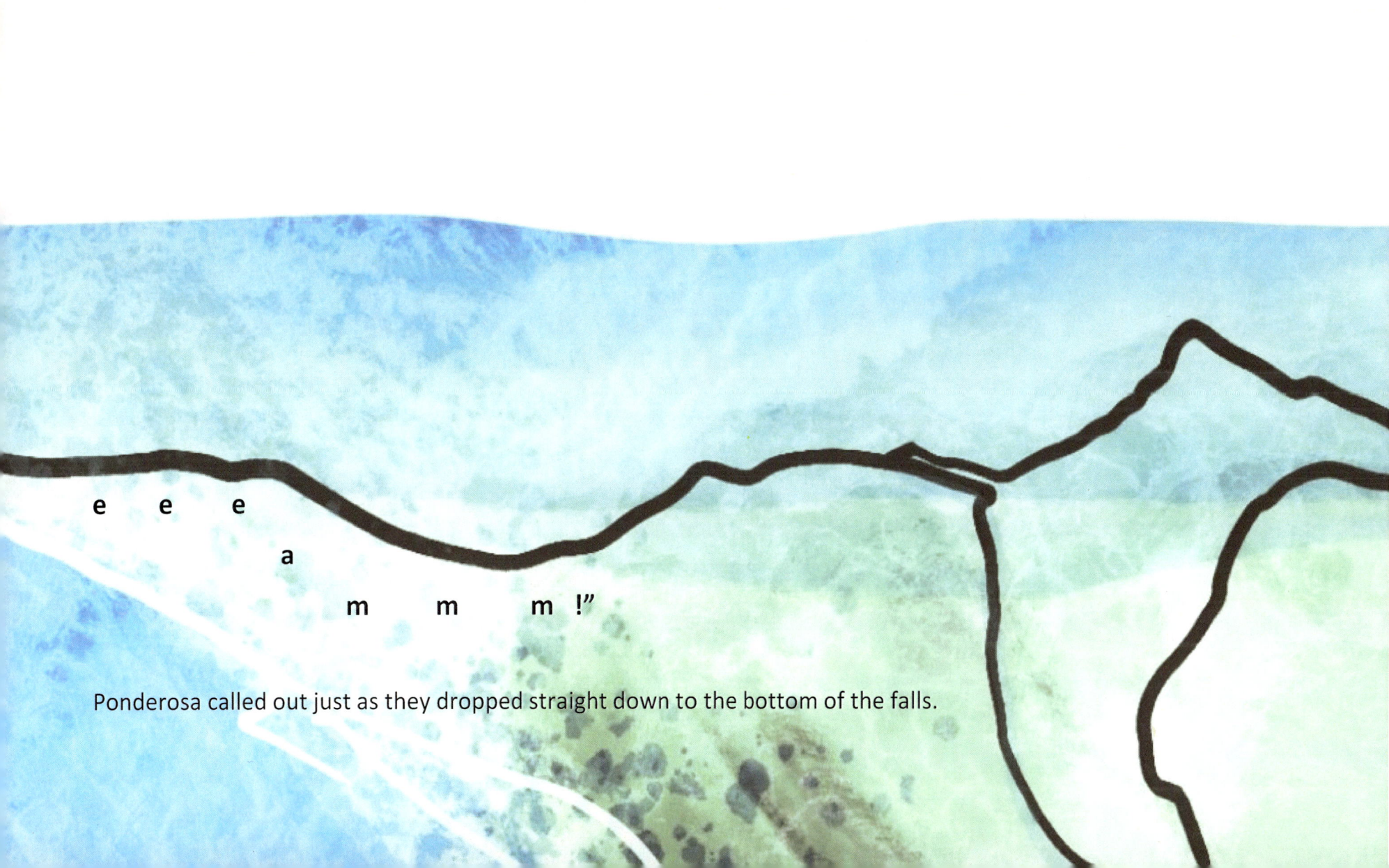

e e e
a
m m m !"

Ponderosa called out just as they dropped straight down to the bottom of the falls.

They landed with a loud KERSPLASH! Ponderosa bobbed and bounced ever downstream. The wild river slowly became more and more gentle. Rosie caught her breath; she was shaking all over. She opened her eyes and saw so many new things! Purple lupine, white yarrow, tiny yellow roses, just like her, and sky-blue forget-me-nots. It was all so beautiful. She thought she could even hear the distant voices of children. Could this be? Then she remembered Father Sun's words:

"Tiny rose so pink and bright,

Your petals open to the light.

The river flows beneath your branch,

Running, leaping, in its dance!

You long to see what lies beyond,

Perhaps you'll find a quiet pond?

Brave as the river,

From here on after,

Listen for the children's laughter."

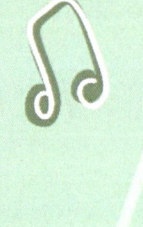

Ponderosa glided into Forget-Me-Not Island with a gentle

bump,

"Here's your stop, Rosie!"

"Thank you for the ride, Ponderosa!" she answered, "Good luck

with the beavers!" Ponderosa waved a branch and floated on

down the river. Mrs. Lizard, who had  also been swept up by the

pine tree, came and sat next to the tiny

pink rose, who was very happy to see her. "That was quite an

adventure,"

Mrs. Lizard said as she wrapped her star-shaped toes softly

around Rosie.

That evening Mrs. Lizard made a cozy nest out of moss and

there she laid her eggs under the

moon and stars.

The next morning a little boy, humming a little tune, rowed his red boat to the small island where he found Rosie sitting amid the forget-me-nots. The boy gently picked the rose up, making a cozy nest with his small hands. He breathed in her sweet scent, the smell of every good thing he had ever known.

Later in the afternoon, Father Sun's warm light bathed Rosie where she rested in the most beautiful crystal water bowl. Her five petals opened wide, like a star. The crystal bowl sat upon a fine wooden table. The fine wooden table was surrounded by a cozy home. The cozy home was well-loved and cared for by the boy and his family. The boy came over often to smell the fragrance of the tiny pink wild rose. Together they closed their eyes and smiled.

**About the Creative Team**

Niki, Taylor, and Margie taught together in the Hummingbird Kindergarten at the Waldorf School of Bend. There, they enjoyed gathering around the snack table with the children over a delicious bowl of "kindergarten soup" and a good story. This book was inspired by their sweet students, and many an outdoor adventure among the beautiful creeks, rivers and waterfalls of Central Oregon.

CPSIA information can be obtained
at www.ICGtesting.com
Printed in the USA
LVRC102153060521
686754LV00003B/46